let's travel in

SPAIN

Edited by Darlene Geis

A TRAVEL PRESS BOOK

PICTURE ACKNOWLEDGMENTS
The illustrations in this book are the work of the following photographers and artists, whose collaboration is gratefully acknowledged. For the full-color pages, Josef Muench (1, 2, 13, 25, 27, 30 and 32); Barnaby's Picture Library (3, 5, 10, 11, 14, 18, 22, 23 and 29); Orville Goldner (4 and 17); P.I.P. (6, 15 and 16); Réalités, from P.I.P. (7, 9 and 12); Yan, from Rapho-Guillumette (8); Ned Haines, from Rapho-Guillumette (20); Elizabeth Moul (19); Larry Colwell, from Photo Researchers, Inc. (21); Herbert Lanks (24); Tom Hollyman, from Photo Researchers, Inc. (26); Fritz Henle, from Photo Researchers, Inc. (28 and 31). For the black-and-white photographs we wish to thank Three Lions; The Bettmann Archive; Inge Morath from Magnum; Brassai, Bernd Lohse, Kit Robbins, Almasy and Bernard Silberstein from Rapho-Guillumette; the Spanish National Tourist Office; and Barnaby's Picture Library.
The map was made by Enrico Arno.

CONTENTS

SPAIN, LAND OF SUNLIGHT AND SHADOW 9

PLAZA IN MADRID: Statue of Don Quixote 16

RETIRO PARK: Royal Estate 18

PROUD PROFESSION: The Bullfighter 21

ROYAL CARPET FACTORY: Fabulous Tapestries 22

PEASANT GIRLS: Costumes of Lagartera 25

BEACH AT SAN SEBASTIAN: Elegant Resort 26

SANTILLANA DEL MAR: Medieval Town 29

SANTIAGO DE COMPOSTELA: Pilgrim City 30

WINDMILL IN LA MANCHA: Quixote's Giant 33

ARCO DE SANTA MARIA: Gateway in Burgos 34

ROMAN AQUEDUCT: Wonder of Segovia 37

CASTLE IN SPAIN: Segovia's Alcazar 38

FORTRESS CITY: Granite-Walled Avila 41

FISHING VILLAGE: The Costa Brava 42

SPAIN'S LARGEST PORT: Busy Barcelona 45

CATALAN ARCHITECTURE: Bold New Style 46

MONASTERY OF MONTSERRAT: Legendary Retreat 49

SKIN DIVING: Island of Majorca 50

MAJORCAN MUSIC: Costumed Singers 53

PASTEBOARD SCULPTURE: Celebration in Valencia 54

FACING AFRICA: The Costa Blanca 57

THE GIRALDA TOWER: Minaret in Seville 58

ANDALUSIAN COSTUMES: Seville's Feria 61

LITTLE PENITENTS: Holy Week Procession 62

MUSEUM CITY: Silent Toledo 65

VINTAGE FIESTA: Harvest Festival 66

PALACE GARDEN: Splendor in Granada 69

GRANADA GYPSIES: Flamenco Dancer 70

COURT OF THE LIONS: The Alhambra 73

DOORMAN IN CORDOVA: Moorish Legacy 74

THE COSTA DEL SOL: Harbor at Málaga 77

SMALL BUT MIGHTY: The Rock of Gibraltar 78

SOME IMPORTANT DATES IN SPANISH HISTORY 80

SOME FAMOUS NAMES IN SPANISH HISTORY 81

SOME SPANISH WORDS AND PHRASES 82

INDEX 83

Bay of Biscay

ATLANTIC OCEAN

PORTUGAL

MEDITER

MOROCCO

Santiago de Campostela **8**

Santillana del Mar **7**

San Sebastián **6**

Burgos **10**

Duero River

Segovia **11-12**

Avila **13**

Lagartera **5**

Madrid **1-4**

Toledo **25**

Guadiana River

LA MANCHA **9**

Seville **22-24**

Cordova **30**

Guadalquivir River

Granada **27-29**

Jerez de la Frontera **26**

Málaga **31**

Algeciras — Gibraltar **32**

Strait of Gibraltar

FRANCE

PYRENEES

Ebro River

17 Montserrat

15-16 Barcelona

14 Tossa de Mar

19 Palma
MAJORCA

20 Valencia

21 Benidorm

18

BALEARIC ISLANDS

MEDITERRANEAN SEA

UNA · GRANDE · LIBRE
PLUS ULTRA

ALGERIA

Locales of thirty-two full-color pictures

1. PLAZA IN MADRID:
   Statue of Don Quixote p. 17

2. RETIRO PARK:
   Royal Estate p. 19

3. PROUD PROFESSION:
   The Bullfighter p. 20

4. ROYAL CARPET FACTORY:
   Fabulous Tapestries p. 23

5. PEASANT GIRLS:
   Costumes of Lagartera p. 24

6. BEACH AT SAN SEBASTIAN:
   Elegant Resort p. 27

7. SANTILLANA DEL MAR:
   Medieval Town p. 28

8. SANTIAGO DE COMPOSTELA:
   Pilgrim City p. 31

9. WINDMILL IN LA MANCHA:
   Quixote's Giant p. 32

10. ARCO DE SANTA MARIA:
    Gateway in Burgos p. 35

11. ROMAN AQUEDUCT:
    Wonder of Segovia p. 36

12. CASTLE IN SPAIN:
    Segovia's Alcazar p. 79

13. FORTRESS CITY:
    Granite-Walled Avila p. 40

14. FISHING VILLAGE:
    The Costa Brava p. 43

15. SPAIN'S LARGEST PORT:
    Busy Barcelona p. 44

16. CATALAN ARCHITECTURE:
    Bold New Style p. 47

17. MONASTERY OF MONTSERRAT:
    Legendary Retreat p. 48

18. SKIN DIVING:
    Island of Majorca p. 51

19. MAJORCAN MUSIC:
    Costumed Singers p. 52

20. PASTEBOARD SCULPTURE:
    Celebration in Valencia p. 55

21. FACING AFRICA:
    The Costa Blanca p. 56

22. THE GIRALDA TOWER:
    Minaret in Seville p. 59

23. ANDALUSIAN COSTUMES:
    Seville's Feria p. 60

24. LITTLE PENITENTS:
    Holy Week Procession p. 63

25. MUSEUM CITY:
    Silent Toledo p. 64

26. VINTAGE FIESTA:
    Harvest Festival p. 67

27. PALACE GARDEN:
    Splendor in Granada p. 68

28. GRANADA GYPSIES:
    Flamenco Dancer p. 71

29. COURT OF THE LIONS:
    The Alhambra p. 72

30. DOORMAN IN CORDOVA:
    Moorish Legacy p. 75

31. THE COSTA DEL SOL:
    Harbor at Málaga p. 76

32. SMALL BUT MIGHTY:
    The Rock of Gibraltar p. 79

SPAIN,

LAND OF SUNLIGHT AND SHADOW

WHEN you cross the mountains that divide France from Spain you step into another world. "Europe ends at the Pyrenees" (PIHR-*eh-neez*), said Napoleon, and it is true that the land beyond the mountains has a character and personality that are strikingly different. The sun beats down mercilessly on a country that, in large part, is closer akin to Africa than to its own continent.

The Iberian (*eye*-BEER-*ih-uhn*) Peninsula is tacked onto the southwest corner of Europe by a band of mountains whose average height is higher than that of the Alps. Behind that wall of the Pyrenees the peninsula is stretched in a rough square—"the bull's hide," it was called in an ancient treaty. Portugal occupies a narrow rectangle on the Atlantic, and the remaining 190,000 square miles belong to Spain. It is a harsh land of violent contrasts, and each region has its own distinctive flavor.

The hot winds of Africa blow across southwestern Spain. There, sun-bleached white houses and palm trees reflect the continent that lies just ten miles to the south, across the Strait of Gibraltar. Northwestern Spain, curving into the Atlantic, is a Spanish Ireland with its misty green mountains and blue bays, and people who, like the Irish, are of Celtic origin. The high Castilian tableland is as stern and unsmiling as its proud inhabitants. Here, at the heart of Spain, is that most Spanish of landscapes—the stark and almost treeless plain, tawny hills, harsh sunlight, black shadows, and a vast and empty loneliness resembling the surrealistic scenes of Salvador Dali (DAH-*lee*), the Spanish painter.

Isolated by a mountainous seacoast and by the rugged Pyrenees, Spain is also a land of isolated regions within its borders. Ranges of mountains carve the country into separate areas, and the fierce individualism of the Spaniards is due in large part to their country's geography. Spain has been cut off from the mainstream of European history, but its people still remember the days of their country's past greatness.

THE FAMILY TREE

The Spaniards' pride of ancestry can go back thousands of years to the Stone Age hunters who once roamed the Iberian Peninsula. These prehistoric men left caves decorated with remarkable paintings of the animals they hunted—deer, bison, horses, wild boar—who charge across

9

the walls today, lively masterpieces 16,000 years old. The cavemen who created them were the first in a long and illustrious line of Spanish painters that includes Velázquez (*veh*-LATH-*keth*), El Greco (*ehl* GREH-*koh*), Goya (GOH-*yah*) and, in our day, Picasso (*pee*-KAH-*soh*).

About 3000 years ago, Celtic tribes burst through the western passes of the Pyrenees and poured across northern and western Iberia. Mean-

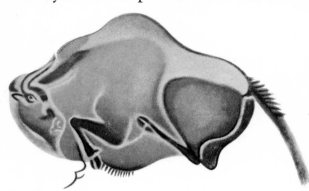

The cave paintings at Altamira look fresh and modern after thousands of years.

while, the Mediterranean coast was visited by Phoenician and Greek trading ships, and later by Carthaginians from North Africa. In the third and second centuries B.C., Rome became the great Mediterranean power. Carthage was wiped out by Roman forces in the Punic (PEW-*nick*) Wars and the Romans sent their legions to Spain where they spent many costly years subduing the stubborn mountain people. The dogged resistance of these early Spaniards was epitomized by the little city of Numantia (*new*-MAN-*shuh*) which held off the Romans for twenty years. When it finally fell to 60,000 besiegers, the Romans paid tribute to its valor with these words, "a small city but immense in glory."

ROMAN SPAIN

By 19 B.C. Rome had tamed the whole peninsula and it was to put its lasting mark on Spain. Roman law and Christianity were adopted by the Spaniards. The Romans introduced the Latin language, which became the root of Castilian Spanish; the mountainous land was crisscrossed with 18,000 miles of Roman roads; towering aqueducts arched across the arid plains; amphitheaters, circuses, bridges, sewer and heating systems brought the comforts of an advanced civilization to the country that the Romans called Hispania (*his*-PAY-*nih-uh*)—from which its present name derives.

In return, Spain gave Rome the wealth of its mines—gold, silver, copper, tin, lead and iron. And it furnished the empire with valiant Spanish soldiers who fought in the Roman legions, two emperors—Hadrian (HAY-*drih-an*) and Trajan (TRAY-*jan*)—and the important Latin writers Seneca (SEHN-*eh-kuh*), Martial (MAHR-*shahl*) and Juvenal (JOO-*veh-n'l*).

But after nearly 650 years of Roman influence, Spain, with the rest of the crumbling empire, fell prey to the barbarians. The Visigoths ruled in Spain from the fifth to eighth centuries, but the only memento of their stay is an occasional blond or redheaded Spaniard, some traces of the Visigoths' legal code, and a few of their words that seeped into Spanish. The Visigoths were not very capable rulers, and by 711 A.D. Spain was ready to fall like a ripe fig to the Berbers of North Africa.

EIGHT HUNDRED MOSLEM YEARS

The Moorish centuries began in 711 with the landing of Tariq (TAH-*rick*) the One-Eyed and his infidel hordes at Gibraltar. In the beginning they were helped by the treachery of some of the Visigoth nobles, and after the Visigoth king was killed in battle, the African invaders streamed northward. They were halted in the wild highlands of Asturias (*ahs*-TOO-*ryahs*), where some of the fleeing Visigoths had set up a Christian kingdom. This mountainous section of northern Spain was to become the stronghold of the Christian reconquest, a separate kingdom which was dedicated, for eight hundred years, to driving the Moors out of Spain.

But eight centuries is a long, long time, and much that is splendid, colorful and exotic in Spain today flowered from the deeply rooted Moorish civilization of those years. The columns and arches of many of the buildings, cloistered gardens with their tinkling fountains, the wailing overtones of the East in Spanish music, carpets, embossed leather, metalwork, ceramics—all of these things that we think of as distinctively Spanish have a strong Moorish cast to them.

While Moslem Spain grew soft through centuries of wealth and oriental luxury, the Christian section of the country was never more firmly united. Furthermore it was toughened and strengthened by a fanatical zeal to reconquer and Christianize all of Spain. Over the years the Christian kingdom had expanded. León (*lay*-OWN), Aragon and Castile were united under Ferdinand and Isabella, and in 1492 the last Moorish stronghold at Granada fell to the "Catholic Sovereigns," as they were called.

CONQUEST AND DECLINE

In that same fateful year Spain not only reclaimed all of its own land from the Moors, it was also presented with a whole new world to conquer by Columbus. The hunger for reconquest and the militant religious zeal that had been developed in the long fight against Islam found new outlets in the conquest of America and the Spanish Inquisition.

Unfortunately, Spain had not had time enough to stabilize itself as a unified country when its daring sailors and explorers gave it a vast colonial empire. The gold and wealth of America flowed into Spain, only

11

to be poured out again on foreign battlefields and in foreign markets that supplied products not produced at home. "Spain eats the New World, but it is the Low Countries that grow fat on it," was a saying that pointed up the hidden weakness of Spain's golden century.

The disintegration of Spain's empire began with the wreckage of the Invincible Armada in British waters, and from 1588 on, Spanish fortunes slid downhill. In the intervening years Spain has been ruled by Hapsburgs, briefly by Joseph Bonaparte and by the Bourbons. It has survived more than a hundred years of governmental chaos, culminating in the brutal Civil War of 1936-39.

A million lives were lost as Spaniard fought against Spaniard, and the country became a battleground for the conflicting ideologies of Communism and Fascism with foreign intervention on both sides. In 1939 the Republican government forces surrendered to the Nationalist rebels led by General Francisco Franco, who has ruled Spain ever since. In 1947 Spain declared itself a kingdom, and General Franco's successor some day will be a qualified member of the Bourbon royal family, decided upon by the government.

THE PROUD PEOPLE

You must see the Spaniard against the background of his history in order to understand him. Although much of Spain is poverty-stricken, even the poorest Spaniard carries himself with pride and honor. This is one country where the tourist will find he need not worry about being cheated. The fierce Spanish integrity will brook no dishonesty. Every man, rich or poor, considers himself a *caballero* (kah-bahl-YEH-roh), a gentleman, whose memory of his country's past greatness is reflected in his unfailing courtesy and sense of honor.

Appearances are very important, and men and women will stint on other things in order to be well-dressed. Shiny shoes are almost a national trademark, especially in the cities where rows of shoeshine boys do a thriving business on the sidewalks. In the old days you could recognize a *caballero* (which originally meant "horseman") by his polished boots, which proved that he never had to go on foot along Spain's dusty roads. Today there is little or no class distinction in this land where every man is a gentleman. There are, however, regional differences that are strongly marked, but the Spanish ideals of valor and chivalry are common to all.

THE MANY FACES OF SPAIN

Traveling through the country, your first impression is of the parched brown earth, punctuated here and there with a hilltop castle rising

12

nobly above empty fields. There are more than fourteen hundred castles in Spain, and they cast a spell of romance over even the most barren land.

Spaniards still think of their country in terms of its ancient kingdoms and counties, and the nine main regions retain their distinct character. Galicia (*gah*-LISH-*yuh*), the wet and mountainous "Irish" corner of Spain, has its own language, and its people have been characterized as "sensual, melancholic, poetic, superstitious"—and shrewd.

In the northern mountains of Asturias, the Cradle of Spanish Independence, you can still see the cave where the Visigoth leaders gathered to plot their stand against the Moorish invaders. The men and women of Asturias are frequently tall, blond and blue-eyed, and among the handsomest in the country, though not typically Spanish-looking.

Navarre (*nah*-VAHR), across the Pyrenees from France, is the home of the Basques (BASKS) who are believed to be the survivors of prehistoric Iberians, driven by later invaders into the mountains. Their language is an ancient tongue-twister, their customs, songs, sports and the people's sturdy toughness are quite unlike anything else in Spain.

Spanish cities of the south still have the balconies and narrow streets of Moorish times.

Slicing into the Pyrenees next to Navarre is the region that used to be the old kingdom of Aragon. "The Aragonese," says an old proverb, "are obstinate enough to hammer nails with their heads." Christians and Arabs battled over Aragon, and its people still have a fighting determination to protect their liberty, their faith and their pride. Catalonia (*cat-uh*-LONE-*yuh*), the northeastern corner of Spain, has a wildly beautiful Mediterranean coast, and a people who also have their own language. The Catalans are hard-working and clever—"They can squeeze bread out of a stone," according to a Spanish proverb. Barcelona, the Catalan capital, is the second largest and the wealthiest city of Spain, its industry and commerce making it the mainstay of the Spanish economy.

For the dark, flashing-eyed Spaniard of the fiery temperament you must go to Andalusia and Estremadura (*ess-treh-mah*-DOO-*ruh*), the Spanish south and southwest. Here the ancient Mediterranean civilizations melted together under the blazing sun, and here the Moors built their fabulous citadels. This is the poorest, yet the gayest part of Spain.

THE SPANISH HEARTLAND

The central plateau of León and Castile is the land of the Spaniard whom most of us think of as typical—stern, austere, unbending, yet so overwhelmingly courteous that the harsh character is softened. Castilian Spanish is the national language and it is spoken in its purest form in this region, though the language, with modifications, was carried to Spain's vast colonial holdings. Today it is the mother tongue of some 85,000,000 people—nearly three times the number of Spain's inhabitants.

At the heart of Castile and almost at the center of Spain, rising from the desolate plateau like an improbable vision, is the modern metropolis of Madrid. The capital of Spain seems to be the least Spanish of cities— much of it has been rebuilt in the twentieth century, borrowing styles from Europe and the United States that are alien to this land. Compared with Toledo, Cadiz (*kuh*-DIHZ) or Cordova (KOR-*doh-vuh*), whose histories go back several thousand years, Madrid is a newcomer. It has been Spain's capital since the sixteenth century, but only in the past twenty years has Madrid become the undisputed center of the nation culturally, administratively and in the hearts of the people.

We will start our tour of Spain in Madrid, for while other towns are all very typical of their province—they are Andalusian, Catalan or Aragonese—it is in Madrid alone that one finds the essence of Spain itself.

A man can transact business, get his shoes shined and enjoy the fresh air at sidewalk cafés in Madrid.

let's travel in
SPAIN

PLAZA IN MADRID: STATUE OF DON QUIXOTE

MADRID is out to prove that, though it is officially classed only as a town, it deserves the rank of city. This twentieth-century metropolis is modern Spain, yet its old quarters speak of earlier times, and it is in Madrid that we find the cultural heritage of the nation enshrined. The great painters of Spain's past are represented with a wealth of glowing canvases in the Prado (PRAH-*doe*), Madrid's famous museum.

And here, in the Plaza de España (PLAH-*thah deh es-*PAH-*nyah*), is a monument to the seventeenth-century writer Cervantes (*thehr-*VAHN-*tess*) and his immortal characters Don Quixote (*dohn kee-*HOH-*teh*) and Sancho Panza (SAHN-*choh* PAHN-*thah*). The dreamy, impractical knight and his peasant squire with his rough wisdom seem to embody the chief traits of the Spanish temperament. "All Spaniards," according to an old saying, "have in them a little of Quixote, something of the poet, and a good deal of the bullfighter."

Towering behind the monument is one of the tallest buildings in Europe, the Edificio España (*eh-dee-*FEETH-*yoh es-*PAH-*nyah*). Madrid has a number of modern skyscrapers, for most of the city has been built in recent times. Until 1936 it was much the same as it had been since the eighteenth century. Then in the civil war it was besieged for three years. During the siege a Nationalist general said that he had four columns of soldiers converging on Madrid and a "fifth column" of sympathizers within the city. Thus a new phrase was born.

After the civil war the bombed city was rebuilt, and the new, strongly centralized government made Madrid its headquarters. The population doubled in twenty years—there are nearly two million *Madrileños* (*mah-dree-*LEN-*yohs*) now—and hotels, restaurants, shops and government buildings mushroomed from the bombed ruins. The Gran Via (*grahn* VEE-*ah*), Madrid's finest shopping street, leads to this plaza. Yet, in the very shadow of these skyscrapers, just off the Gran Via, you will find the narrow streets, old houses and mellow churches of another age.

16

RETIRO PARK: ROYAL ESTATE

NEAR the center of Madrid a spacious park spreads across 350 pleasant acres. Gardens, children's playgrounds, bridle paths, a zoo and this broad lake make it one of the favorite summertime retreats for *Madrileños*. Their city is two thousand feet above sea level, surrounded by a wind-swept plain. Consequently Madrid's climate has been described as "nine months of winter, three months of hell."

In the searing heat of summer, shady Retiro (*reh*-TEE-*roh*) Park with its fountains and lake is thronged with people. They stroll along its cool paths, or enjoy a drink and a snack at one of the outdoor cafés. The park and gardens were carved out of a dense forest that once surrounded old Madrid. Philip II built a palace there for his English queen, Mary Tudor, and until 1869 Retiro was the scene of many a royal fête. Then, in the reign of King Alfonso XII, it was presented to Madrid as a public park. A monument to the generous king stands at the water's edge.

Retiro Park is not the only place in town where one may enjoy the outdoors. Madrid's animated citizens can be found before lunch or in the late afternoon sitting at café tables along the elegant boulevards. Spain runs on a different schedule from most other countries, and Madrid's streets reflect the unusual timetable. Shops and offices are closed from one to four p.m. Lunch is seldom eaten before two or three. A movie or theatre matinee starts at six-thirty, while evening performances begin at eleven. And in Madrid the dinner hour is ten-thirty at the earliest.

The long hours between meals, when there is nothing else to do, can be whiled away in the hundreds of hospitable cafés in Madrid. They serve as clubs or even as offices, where a man can spend several hours over a cup of coffee, transact business, send a messenger boy on errands, and indulge in the favorite pastime of the *Madrileño*—conversation. No one watches the clock in this delightful city except for one event— the bullfight—which starts promptly and is taken seriously.

PROUD
PROFESSION:
THE
BULLFIGHTER

BULLFIGHTING is more than a sport in Spain. It is the national art of a people who respect courage and gallantry above all. The age-old spirit of conquest has its expression now in the graceful and daring figure of the matador subduing a wild and dangerous beast. Each time the drama is played out on the sandy floor of a bull ring the audience watches, not the dreary spectacle of an animal being slaughtered, but the solemn rite of man's mastery over fear and over death itself.

When a matador like the one in this picture struts proudly into the bull ring, he knows fear. He knows that his chance of meeting death in the ring is one out of ten. And the odds are one to four that he will be seriously wounded. Under the flashing "suit of lights" the bullfighter's body is scarred from old encounters with the bull's sharp horns. Yet there is scarcely a boy growing up in Spain who does not long to be a *torero* (*toh-*REH*-roh*). You can see urchins training in the streets with a ragged jacket for a cape and a friend to play the part of the charging bull. It is a dangerous career, but one of the few in which a Spanish boy can achieve wealth and honor today. The top matadors make as much as forty thousand dollars for an afternoon's work at Madrid's Plaza de Toros (TOH-*rohs*). In threadbare Spain, the brave man dressed in the rich embroidery of a matador is a national hero.

These sandlot bullfighters practice to acquire skill, but for the real thing they must be born brave.

ROYAL CARPET FACTORY: FABULOUS TAPESTRIES

THE glittering costume of the matador originated in the late eighteenth century at almost the same time that Spanish tapestries reached their high point of artistry. Both owed something to the great painter Francisco Goya. Goya led a turbulent life, and at one time he was a member of a troupe of traveling bullfighters. His interest in the sport resulted in a series of brilliant paintings and in a group of wax matador statuettes whose costumes Goya is believed to have designed.

The Santa Barbara factory in Madrid, famous for its tapestries and carpets, hired Goya when he was still a struggling young artist to create cartoons—the paintings from which tapestries are woven—for them. Goya's designs were lively scenes of village and farm life which found immediate favor with the royal family. Goya went on to become the favorite court painter of his time, and the Santa Barbara factory produced its greatest masterpieces from his vivid and dramatic paintings.

In this picture we are watching a weaver at work on one of the colorful and complicated tapestries. He is sitting behind a vertical loom, and the main outlines of his design are drawn directly on the warps—the long white strands on which the colored wool is woven. The weaver usually works from the back of his tapestry, with a mirror facing the finished side. He can peer through the unwoven warps and watch his work in progress, checking it against the large painting beside him which he is reproducing in tapestry.

Each different color of wool is wound around a separate bobbin. Tapestry is unlike any other kind of weaving in that the horizontal threads are not woven clear across the web each time. Instead, each color is woven only over the area where it appears in the design. It is an enormously complicated process. Yet, miraculously, the living figure of a peasant girl is emerging from the screen of threads, and she and her basket of oranges seem more real than the weaver who is creating them.

PEASANT GIRLS: COSTUMES OF LAGARTERA

ON SUNDAYS and at festivals the girls of Spain are dressed as picturesquely as the figures in the old tapestries. Each colorful region has its own costume, and the striking differences in climate, landscape, customs and language of the various sections of Spain are emphasized by the wide variety of their holiday dress.

These girls are from the village of Lagartera (*lah-gar-*TEH*-rah*) in Castile. It is an ordinary little town of spotlessly whitewashed cottages, but it is famous throughout Spain for the splendor and distinctiveness of its costumes. The outfit looks more Hungarian than Spanish, but actually it was influenced by the Moors. The embroidered cloths and scarves that cover the head are found nearly all over Spain—a reminder of the veiled ladies of Islam. And the brilliantly knitted stockings that these girls wear are the counterpart of the slippers and leggings that Berber shepherds used to knit for themselves during the long hours of watching their flocks on the mountains.

A wedding in Lagartera is a sight to behold. The girls dance and twirl and their layers of gorgeous skirts spin out like a ballerina's costume. All week long they may have to grub in the fields wearing shabby old clothes, but on the special occasions when they don their traditional finery and perform their ancient dances, the ladies of Spain live up to their reputation for beauty.

In Andalusia the women dress in Gypsy ruffles and proudly show off their long full skirts.

BEACH AT SAN SEBASTIAN: ELEGANT RESORT

THERE has always been enormous wealth in Spain as well as incredible poverty, another of the sharp contrasts in this land of light and shadow. The great feudal estates that total nearly half of Spain are owned by only one hundredth of the population, and most of the proprietors are absentee landlords who do not want to live in rural isolation. Fashionable resorts like San Sebastián show us this wealthy and pleasure-loving side of Spain.

Situated on the northern coast, only twelve miles from the French border, San Sebastián was for years the summer residence of the Spanish court. It is still the official seat of the Spanish government from July until October, and to add to its cosmopolitan smartness, members of all the embassies in Madrid set up summer headquarters at this delightful watering place. A cool sea breeze blows from the Bay of Biscay onto the shell-shaped curve of beach called La Concha (*lah* KOHN-*chah*). But there is more to do in San Sebastián than this picture would indicate. This is the rugged Basque country where outdoor sports are an enthusiastic way of life. Daily bullfights, boxing, horse racing, golf, tennis and yachting take up the off-beach hours. Pigeon shooting is popular here too, but not with Anglo-Saxons who feel the odds against the pigeon are unsporting. And there is always the fascinating opportunity to explore the romantic Basque country when the game-playing palls.

Café tables under the trees are part of the holiday charm of San Sebastián.

SANTILLANA DEL MAR: MEDIEVAL TOWN

WESTWARD along the Biscay coast, about a hundred miles from San Sebastián, the world of fashion gives way to the Middle Ages when we stand on the cobbled streets of Santillana del Mar (*sahn-teel-*YAH*-nah del mar*). The village dates from the twelfth century when it was founded around the Monastery of Santa Juliana (SAHN-*tah* hool-YAH-*nah*), a Spanish saint whose name, pronounced in the local manner, is the name of the town.

Unchanged for the past four hundred years, Santillana is now a national monument of Spain. Not a house nor a building may be altered, the streets must remain unpaved, and the village must forego such innovations as movie houses and television aerials. Cows' hoofs ring on the cobblestones as they have all through the town's history, and at the entrance to the twelfth-century church, an iron grille on the ground prevents cattle from stepping into the sacred precincts.

Santillana was the home town of one of Spain's most beloved literary rogues. The sharp-witted Gil Blas (*heel blahss*) set out from this quiet village to make his rascally fortune, and the local inn has been named after him. Santillana is also the place where some of the noblest families in Spain originated. Many of the simple, whitewashed houses carry impressive coats-of-arms over their doorways, reminding the visitor that the aristocracy of old Castile sprang from these modest beginnings.

Two miles from Santillana we are cast back even further in time— maybe eleven thousand, maybe even twenty thousand years before the Christian era. Under a green hillside are the wondrous Caves of Altamira (AHL-*tah*-ME-*rah*) where men, dressed in the skins of wild animals, lived and left a record of their prehistoric world. Their cave paintings, originally seen by flickering firelight, glow now in the bright beams of electric lamps. A French *abbé*, who saw the painted caves some years ago, marveled and called them "The Sistine Chapel of the Ice Age."

SANTIAGO DE COMPOSTELA: PILGRIM CITY

IN A COUNTRY where many magnificent cathedrals tower against the sky, this one in the remote northwest province of Galicia is the most remarkable. For it is here, within this twin-spired monument, that the remains of St. James the Apostle repose in a carved silver box. He had been a missionary in Spain for seven years, and later, after his martyrdom in Judea (*joo*-DEE-*uh*), his disciples brought his body back to the wild hills of Galicia that he had loved so well. Six hundred years later, in the ninth century, a bright star and the sound of angelic music guided people to a field where the saint's remains were found.

A small church was built on the spot, called *Campus Stellae* (KAHM-*poos* STEH-*leh*) or Field of the Star, from which we get Compostela. Not long after, a vision of St. James riding a white horse appeared to the Christian forces engaged in a desperate battle against the Moorish invaders. The Christians won the battle, and Saint James became the patron saint of Spain. From then on *"Santiago!"*—his Spanish name— was the battle cry of the soldiers of the reconquest, and it was heard in America when Spanish troops rode against the pagan Incas and Aztecs.

The Cathedral of Santiago that we see here is one of the oldest and largest churches in Spain. It was begun in the eleventh century, but additions were made to it for seven hundred years. Santiago de Compostela, remote though it is, is a city of more than 50,000 inhabitants. It is the holiest place in Spain, and during the Middle Ages it ranked with Rome and Jerusalem as a shrine for pilgrims. They trudged on foot across France and Spain, carrying the cockleshell of St. James and a pilgrim's staff, and many kings of far countries were among the wayfarers. Even now on July 25, the feast day of St. James, the cathedral square is thronged with pilgrims. The statue of the saint looks down upon the square from its niche in the central tower, and Galician mountaineers in ancient costumes dance to the tune of bagpipes, much as they might have done when St. James preached here.

WINDMILL IN LA MANCHA: QUIXOTE'S GIANT

SOUTH of Madrid the Castilian plateau is bare and dry. This is the region known as La Mancha (*lah* MAHN-*chah*), a name that comes from the Arabic word meaning "arid." The fame of this dusty plain has spread to many countries, for it was here that Cervantes' immortal hero, Don Quixote of La Mancha, rode forth to his ridiculous but endearing adventures. The Don was a middle-aged man, gaunt and thin, who had lost his wits from reading too many stories of chivalry. He rode about the barren countryside wearing his great-grandfather's suit of armor, and following him on a donkey was his squire, Sancho Panza, always ready with a Spanish proverb or some common-sense advice.

At one point Quixote saw a group of windmills like this one, and charged at them full tilt, convinced that they were giants waving their arms at him. In vain Sancho Panza called out the truth, but the Don and his scrawny horse were flattened by one of the revolving vanes. The phrase "tilting at windmills" has passed over into our language now to mean fighting against imaginary wrongs. Spain has always kept one foot in the past, and it was this reluctance to face modern times that Cervantes was making fun of in his story of the foolish knight.

That was four hundred years ago, and though Spaniards have taken the hero to their hearts, they still cling to the past. The same stone towers with their latticed vanes stand on the plain of La Mancha today, creaking in the wind, centuries removed from the age of the atom.

Giants from times long past are paraded for special celebrations in towns where the old ways still live.

33

ARCO DE SANTA MARIA: GATEWAY IN BURGOS

IN THE Middle Ages, Burgos (BOOR-*gohss*) was the capital of Old Castile, and the city is rich with history. It was the early home of Spain's national hero, the Cid (SIHD), and at Burgos, Ferdinand and Isabella gave Columbus a royal reception when he returned from his second voyage. The triumphal arch in this picture was built to honor Emperor Charles V. The citizens of Burgos had joined in an uprising against the Hapsburg monarch, but when the uprising was suppressed they made this magnificent gesture of apology to appease his wrath. The colossal arch is decorated with statues of Castilian notables including the Cid, and to flatter Charles V, his likeness, too, was placed in the central niche. At the very top, in a separate niche, the Madonna (Santa María) and Child look down at the Bridge of Santa María which leads to the arch.

You pass through this gateway to reach the magnificent Cathedral of Burgos, elaborate even for a Spanish church, its interior glittering with gold from Mexico. Although the first stone was laid in 1221, the cathedral was centuries in the building. Within its massive walls are the tombs of the Cid and his wife, and though much of the hero's life is legendary, his brilliant deeds did flame across eleventh-century Spain, lighting up its history.

The Moors gave him the title *sidi*, "lord." And it is said that when he died near Valencia (*vuh*-LEN-*shuh*), a city which he had conquered, his wife placed his body across his favorite horse and passed with it right through the Moorish ranks. They fell back terror-struck, as they had done before the onslaughts of the living Cid so often in the past. Burgos continues to honor the memory of her greatest son, for this is a hero both of fact and fiction. The epic poem that was written in the twelfth century is a classic of Spanish literature, and the proud bold character of the Castilian soldier of fortune has become the national ideal.

ROMAN AQUEDUCT: WONDER OF SEGOVIA

HISTORY is written in the stones of Spain, and this marvelous aqueduct tells of Roman might 2000 years ago. Legend has it that a servant girl of Segovia(*seh*-нон-*vyah*), complaining of her daily trip to the spring to fetch water, offered her soul to the devil if he could make her task easier. In three hours he raised this astonishing aqueduct, and that is why it is called the Devil's Bridge.

Actually the Roman engineers' feat seems almost as miraculous as the legend, when we look at the aqueduct today. The massive granite stones are laid one upon the other so cleverly that not an ounce of mortar had to be used to hold them together. This is one of the best preserved examples of Roman architecture in the world. The aqueduct joins two hills, and its rows of arches stretch for nearly half a mile, towering over 90 feet high where the ground dips. It carried water into Segovia from the hills until recently, and the people used to say, "Above flows water; wine below," because of the wine shops that clustered at the bases of the granite pillars. The aqueduct is unused today except by hundreds of crows who nest in its masonry. They are the carefree heirs of mighty Roman builders.

Roman road companies might have played in this handsome theater built in the faraway colony of Hispania.

CASTLE IN SPAIN: SEGOVIA'S ALCAZAR

WHO has not dreamed of a castle in Spain? And here it is, the perfect dream castle, rising like the prow of a ship above this rocky stream in Segovia. This region is famous for a number of historic and well-preserved castles that bring to life the romantic past of Castile. But the Alcazar (*ahl*-KAH-*thar*), the turreted fortress-palace that we see here, is one of the most dramatic. Its bold beauty is set off by the rocky cliff that lifts it more than 200 feet above Segovia.

The city has played an important role in the history of Spain. Its early Celtic and Iberian inhabitants tried to hold off the Roman conquerors. But the Romans destroyed the city in 80 B.C. and then rebuilt it for themselves. This castle on its strategic cliff was erected over pre-Roman fortifications. At one time it was the home of Queen Isabella who was proclaimed queen here in 1474. One wonders whether Isabella, high in her shiplike castle, had dreams too, emboldening her to pawn her jewels to back Columbus' enterprise.

Not far from Segovia is one of the showplaces of Spain, the royal hunting lodge of La Granja (*lah* GRAHN-*hah*). The first Bourbon king of Spain, Philip V, dreamed of building a French palace to remind him of his French grandfather's glorious Versailles (*vehr*-SIGH). However, while he was away, Philip's wife decided to surprise him, and she elaborated on his plans with extravagant gardens, cascades and sculptured fountains. When Philip came home after a long absence and saw the formal gardens and the fountains playing in the Spanish wilderness—and saw the bills for building them—he grumbled, "It has cost me three millions and has amused me three minutes." Spoken like any husband anywhere.

FORTRESS CITY: GRANITE-WALLED AVILA

THE battlements of Avila (AH-*vee-lah*) rise from the windswept wastes in an almost perfect state of preservation. This was an ancient Roman city, bitterly fought over for three centuries by Moors and Christians. Then, in the eleventh century, Alfonso VI of Castile brought settlers from other provinces to Avila. Among them were a number of master builders, and for nine years a force of 3000 men labored to rebuild the battered Roman walls into the mightiest fortifications of medieval Spain. They did their work so well that the walls, forty feet high and ten feet thick, still girdle the city without a break nearly 900 years later.

Avila is famous as the birthplace of Spain's great sixteenth-century saint, Santa Teresa. A convent stands on the site of her home, and some of her relics are kept there, among them the saint's walking stick. For Santa Teresa, the mystic, in her striving for the way of perfection, used to walk the rock-strewn land barefoot. Traveling to many parts of Spain, the saint founded more than thirty Carmelite convents. Largely because of Santa Teresa's efforts, Avila has become known as "the fortress that flung back the Reformation."

Today, storks nest untidily in the towers and battlements that circle the city. For six months of the year Avila, near the mountain pass of the snowy Central Sierras, is exposed to bitter winter weather. Its ramparts are buried beneath heavy snows, the surrounding hills are icy, and wolves prowl across the plain. Summer or winter the air has a crystal brilliance, and the city is sharply etched against the clear sky. If it were not for that, the traveler would perhaps imagine that what he saw was an illusion, a medieval mirage, for it is hard to believe that such a changeless scene really exists.

FISHING VILLAGE: THE COSTA BRAVA

THE crenelated walls and watchtowers that we see here, warmed by the Mediterranean sun, may remind us of Avila, but the resemblance ends there. This is the Costa Brava (KOHS-*tah* BRAH-*vah*), the Wild Coast of Catalonia, where the jagged shoreline runs almost from Barcelona to the French border, a distance of ninety miles. Far from the sun-parched plains of Castile, the province of Catalonia shows us a different Spain.

Here the unbelievable blue of the Mediterranean dips into hundreds of tiny coves, and crescent beaches are framed by hills fragrant with pine trees. Terraced orchards and vineyards add their sweet smells to the mild air, and the narrow road that twists and climbs and plunges along the rugged coast is an adventure for all the senses. The Costa Brava was, until recently, fairly inaccessible. Since 1951 when roads, transportation and hotel accommodations were improved, more and more travelers have been discovering the wild beauty of the "Riviera of the Future." Although it is becoming a popular summer vacation region, the Costa Brava and its little fishing villages are still unspoiled.

We are looking down on Tossa de Mar (TOH-*sah deh mar*), which means Mound of the Sea. Pulled up on the beach are the gaily painted boats of the fishing fleet. The fishermen live in a cluster of huts down near the waterfront. Up on the cliffs there are larger houses that belong to owners of vineyards, orchards and olive groves. And crowning the headland are the twelfth-century fortifications of the Old Town. All along the Costa Brava you will see watchtowers and fortresses, mostly in ruins, relics of the years of vigilance along this romantic shore. Barbarians, Moors and pirates, each in their time, threatened the peaceful existence of the coastal villages. Now a new invasion promises to destroy that long-cherished peace. Tossa de Mar, with only fifteen hundred inhabitants, has forty hotels and inns packed to capacity all summer long. The watchtowers are no longer manned, and the new invaders are welcomed with open arms.

SPAIN'S LARGEST PORT: BUSY BARCELONA

THE beautiful old seaport of Barcelona is the chief city of Catalonia, the Spanish province marked for its industry, its fighting spirit and commercial energy. This lively and prosperous city is more than 2000 years old, and it saw ancient Greek traders, the army of Hannibal marching eastward to strike at Rome, Romans, Moors, and Frankish invaders. In June, 1493, Columbus was welcomed here by Ferdinand and Isabella after his first historic voyage. In this picture we see a replica of his ship, the *Santa María*, anchored at the inner port.

The special charm of Barcelona is the result of its mild climate and its situation on a fertile plain set in an amphitheater of the coastal mountains. The city has grown from the small section along the waterfront back to the slopes of the surrounding hills. The older quarter with its narrow winding streets is filled with picturesque treasures from the past, but the newer part of town is a bustling commercial center. The ancient city walls were torn down in the last century and replaced with the *Ramblas* (RAHM-*blahss*), a chain of broad boulevards that divides modern Barcelona from the old town. The tree-bordered *Ramblas* begin at the port where a statue of Columbus stands on a tall column. Cafés, theaters and shops line the *Ramblas*, while automobiles and streetcars flow along them. And in the bright sunshine the surging crowds of Barcelona lend the city an atmosphere of cheerful vitality and gaiety.

At the Court of Barcelona, Columbus presented his sovereigns with tattooed Indians and strange treasure from the New World.

CATALAN ARCHITECTURE: BOLD NEW STYLE

CATALONIA prides itself on its individuality—the region has its own language, at one time it had its own laws, and in this century it has agitated to become a separate republic. The desire to be daringly different shows up in a style of architecture that you will find in Barcelona—boldly fanciful, almost weird and unlike anything you can see anywhere else on earth.

The church in this picture is one of the better-known fantasies of the Catalan architect Antonio Gaudí (*gah-oo*-DEE). Barcelona erupts with a number of his strange creations, tortured shapes that veered towards the modernistic as long ago as 1881. That was when Gaudí began this Church of the Sagrada Familia (*sah*-GRAH-*dah fah*-MEE-*lyah*), or Holy Family. It was never finished, and one wonders who would have the unfettered imagination and off-beat inventiveness to bring this design to completion now. Salvador Dali and Pablo Picasso are Catalans, and their unconventional flights of fancy must stem from the same spirit

Near Barcelona the town of Sitges outdoes itself each year with carpets of live blossoms on the narrow streets.

that inspired this unusual building. Gaudí frequently adapted forms and shapes found in nature for his architecture. He built one house in the shape of a breaking wave with undulating roof and curved walls. And one of his apartment buildings on a main street in Barcelona borrows the strange form of the mountain of Montserrat (*mohn-seh*-RAHT) with balconies suggesting its jagged peaks and crags.

MONASTERY OF MONTSERRAT: LEGENDARY RETREAT

ABOUT 25 miles from Barcelona the remarkable mountain of Montserrat rises in a series of saw-toothed peaks. This marvel of nature has inspired many legends—how else explain the towering cones of naked rock that loom like giant figures above the landscape? One early story told that the mass of rock was split into these deep gorges at the very moment that Christ was crucified. Another legend sprang up about the evergreen shrubs that are massed thickly on the lower slopes. They are permitted to bear their leaves perpetually because they are the plants that sheltered Mary and the Holy Child during their flight into Egypt.

Montserrat with its mysterious grandeur has attracted hermits and religious recluses through the ages. In 880 A.D. a Benedictine monastery was founded here. In the monastery church there is a celebrated statue —the Black Virgin of Montserrat, patron saint of Catalonia—which is supposed to have been carved by St. Luke and brought to Spain by St. Peter. It was lost when the Moors invaded Spain, but shepherds found the statue later on this wild mountainside. When they tried to carry it away to their church, the sacred relic became too heavy to move. That is why a church was built here to enshrine it, and the monastery grew up around it.

Before the shrine of the Black Virgin the wounded warrior Ignatius Loyola, founder of the Jesuits, came to lay down his sword and dedicate his life to serving God. Christopher Columbus made a pilgrimage to Montserrat, followed by Indians loaded down with baskets of gold, rare stones and exotic spices from the New World. Now sixty thousand pilgrims and tourists journey here each year, drawn by the unusual combination of natural splendor and rich religious and historic background. As you stroll along this peaceful path in the monastery garden you can hear the music of solemn Gregorian chants drifting over the wall from the Escolania (*es-koh-*LAH-*nyah*), one of the finest choral groups in the world. It is the final perfect touch.

SKIN DIVING:
ISLAND OF
MAJORCA

ONE of the most famous holiday spots in Spain is the island of Majorca (*mah-HOR-kah*) which lies about a hundred miles off the coast of Catalonia in the Mediterranean. It is the largest of the Balearic (*bal-ih-AR-ik*) Islands, and its name comes from the Roman designation, Major. However, even the major island of this group is small—Majorca is about sixty miles long and fifty miles wide.

Basking in the mild Mediterranean climate, Majorca is mountainous and fertile and its terraced orchards produce oranges, lemons, apricots, figs and almonds. In January and February, when other less fortunate lands are frosted with snow, Majorca's landscape is whitened by millions of exquisite flowering trees whose perfume is part of the island's enchantment.

Palma (*PAHL-mah*), the capital of Majorca, is a city of about 130,000 inhabitants. It overlooks a horseshoe-shaped bay, and strung out along the coast beyond the city are a series of perfect bathing beaches and resort hotels. In this picture we see one of the vacation delights of the island. You can anchor your boat in a romantic cove and explore the clear aquamarine depths with a minimum of skin-diving equipment.

When the underwater sights have been seen, there are marvels to behold underground. About forty-five miles from Palma the fabulous Dragon Caves are a spectacular and mysterious subterranean world. The caverns are subtly illuminated, and their strange formations are mirrored in underground lagoons. In one large cave there is a natural amphitheater on the banks of a dark lake. A thousand people can be seated in this shadowy auditorium to hear a concert played by musicians who are rowed across the deep, still water on barges. In the midst of sunny vacation pleasures, Majorca offers the visitor oddly memorable experiences too.

MAJORCAN MUSIC: COSTUMED SINGERS

MAJORCA'S musical fame is not based on its own local songs or musicians. Yet it has become a sort of music lovers' shrine, with sixty or seventy thousand visitors yearly coming to Valldemosa (*vahl-deh-*MOH-*sah*) to pay homage to a great composer. Or maybe they are merely paying homage to romance. Valldemosa is a former monastery, famed as the residence one winter of Frederic Chopin and the lady novelist who called herself George Sand. The composer had consumption and it was hoped that a winter in sunny Majorca would improve his health. But as luck would have it, the weather was unusually bad. Nevertheless, Chopin wrote some of his greatest music here, including most of the twenty-four preludes, two nocturnes, two polonaises and a mazurka. George Sand fared less well. The local people were hostile to the unconventional Frenchwoman who walked around in trousers and she was forced to give up wearing them in public. (Slacks were an unheard-of item of feminine apparel in 1838.)

As you can see in this picture, the Majorcan dresses are more sober and dignified than most Spanish costumes. The islanders wear them only when performing their folk dances on special occasions. At Valldemosa during the tourist season they perform twice a week. Unlike the spirited songs and dances in other parts of Spain, the Majorcans' music is slow and stately, well-suited to the islanders' plain conservative tastes.

The Civil Guards, famous for their discipline, patrol the whole country. But even they relax on Majorca.

PASTEBOARD SCULPTURE: CELEBRATION IN VALENCIA

SPANISH *fiestas*, whether religious or secular, are explosions of color and sound. In a land that is often harsh and drab, and for a people whose lives are not easy, these festivals are a chance to toss care to the wind. In Valencia, the third largest city of Spain, the most important *fiesta* of the year is known as the *fallas* (FAHL-*yahs*), a three-day celebration of the feast of St. Joseph. During those three days the narrow streets of old Valencia and the bright avenues and plazas of the new metropolis are jammed with people.

From March 17 to March 19 enormous *fallas*, statue groups of wax and cardboard, are set up at street corners and in the squares. They are humorous or grotesque caricatures of famous personalities, or satirical jibes at national or international events. The one in this picture has an Eiffel Tower, Statue of Liberty and Big Ben, surmounted by a kneeling camel and driver. The people who mill around the streets of Valencia during the *fiesta* will have plenty of time to figure out the humor intended in each one. Then on midnight of March 19 the *fiesta* reaches its noisy and brilliant climax. To the deafening racket of fireworks is added the roar and crackle of flames as more than a hundred elaborate *fallas* are set on fire. The sky above Valencia glows as bright as the oranges for which this region is famous. In the morning the mess is cleaned up and Valencia goes back to work.

A shop in Valencia sells the bright pottery and gaudy souvenirs typical of southern Spain.

FACING AFRICA: THE COSTA BLANCA

AS YOU travel south along the Mediterranean from Valencia, the coast takes a sudden turn and faces down toward Africa rather than eastward toward Italy. The orange groves and rice fields are replaced by olive and palm trees in a tawny subtropical landscape. This is the Costa Blanca, or White Coast, blazing beneath the same hot sky that arches above North Africa. It extends for about 70 miles from the Peñon de Ifach (*pen*-YOHN *deh ee*-FAHCH), a sort of junior Rock of Gibraltar, to Alicante (*ah-lee*-KAHN-*teh*), an Oriental town whose Moorish castle looks down on a harbor fringed with date palms.

The Costa Blanca has been neglected by tourists until recently, but it is the latest discovery of travelers who like to see lovely places before they are swarming with other travelers. The dazzling white buildings that seem to grow out of the sun-bleached cliff above this beach look Moroccan or Algerian rather than European. This is the little town of Benidorm (*beh-nee*-DORM), which means "sleep well," but it is growing so rapidly as a resort that its days of quiet sleepiness are numbered.

The beach at Benidorm is considered one of the best in Spain, broad and sandy and lapped by the Mediterranean in its gentlest mood. The land along the Costa Blanca is abloom with carnations, and their heavy spicy fragrance is everywhere, even perfuming the local wine. This is part of the richest coast in Spain, and some of the most delicious food comes from this region. Small lobster-like prawns, called *langostinos* (*lahn-goh*-STEE-*nohs*), are caught in these waters and they are served grilled as one of the great regional delicacies. The national dish, known to us as Spanish rice, is called *paella* (*pah*-ELL-*yah*), and it is at its best in this region near Valencia. It is a highly seasoned concoction of saffron-flavored rice, chicken, red peppers and the infinite variety of sea food found here. All this and scenic beaches too!

THE GIRALDA TOWER: MINARET IN SEVILLE

THIS is the Spain of storybook and opera, the romantic Andalusian Spain where ladies on balconies are serenaded by hot-blooded lovers. Here in Seville the composers of the *Barber of Seville, Carmen* and *Don Giovanni* found a background worthy of grand opera. It was no accident. For Seville, capital of Andalusia, is an intoxicating city where golden sun and deep cool shadows create drama on every street.

The balmy fragrance of orange blossoms, the heady scent of jasmine and roses permeate this ancient city where Moorish gardens still grow luxuriantly. The Arabs left their mark here in the narrow streets and the tile patios hidden away from the life of the city. "God gives a house in Seville to those he loves," says an old Spanish proverb. Seen from the sidewalk the houses look ordinary, but when you walk through to the inner court you are in a secret and enchanted garden straight out of the *Arabian Nights.*

The Moors left Seville its most splendid monument, the tower we see rising here at the end of the street. When Ferdinand III drove the Moors out of Seville in the thirteenth century their ancient mosque was destroyed. But the people of Seville could not bear to tear down the beautiful minaret which they had come to love. They added a bell tower to it, topped by a heroic statue of Faith. The slightest breeze turns the great statue which has been named the Giralda (*hee-*RAHL*-dah*), or weathervane.

The mosque was replaced with a cathedral that was begun in 1402. Seville was a wealthy city, and its pride in being freed from the infidels was expressed in this edifice, the largest Gothic building in the world. "Let us erect a monument that will make posterity believe we were mad," the Sevillians decided. Colossal, grandiose, the cathedral stuns the beholder with its immensity and the richness of its decorations. Each day 500 masses are said in the cathedral's 80 chapels, but its bells ring out over the city from this tower that was once a Moorish minaret.

ANDALUSIAN COSTUMES: SEVILLE'S FERIA

SPRING comes to Seville with a colorful fair that has the city in a gay uproar for a week. On a grassy meadow, behind the tobacco factory immortalized in *Carmen*, throngs of people make merry, dressed in the striking costumes of Andalusia. The women's flounced dresses have been adapted from the ruffled skirts worn by the Gypsies, and you see them in every imaginable combination of colors. Cavaliers and their ladies ride around the grounds of the Feria (FEH-*ryah*), the man dressed in the brimmed hat, short jacket and leather trousers that were copied by the Mexican *charros* (and later modified by our cowboys). The girls ride pillion with grace and elegance, their full skirts spread out around them, their dark hair adorned by the traditional flower behind one ear.

The couple in this picture have stopped at what might be called a "drive in" for some refreshment. There are stalls selling soft drinks and cotton candy, shrimps and *langostinos*, as well as Gypsy tents from which the fumes of exotic cookery drift out over the fair grounds. The clacking of castanets and the thrumming of guitars fills the air, and the dances for which Seville is famous are performed with feet stamping in staccato rhythm. And on top of all this excitement there is a bullfight every afternoon, for the Feria of Seville is like the World's Series for the best of the Spanish matadors.

Cowboys on Spanish ranches carry long spears for the dangerous work of herding ferocious bulls.

LITTLE PENITENTS: HOLY WEEK PROCESSION

BEGINNING on Palm Sunday and ending at sunset on Good Friday, Seville is given over to its Holy Week celebration. Somber and theatrical by turns, the processions that make their way through the city streets to the great cathedral are extraordinary spectacles. Each parish has a statue or group of statues representing a station of the cross. The images are sumptuously clothed in robes of embroidered cloth, some of them encrusted with pearls and jewels. They are called *pasos* (PAH-*sohs*), and are mounted on platforms heaped with flowers and ablaze with candles.

The *pasos* are carried through the streets followed by groups of barefoot penitents in long robes with high peaked hoods that mask their faces. Some are dressed in black, some in scarlet, pale blue, crimson, purple or white. The masked and hooded figures moving between the extravagantly decorated *pasos* are like specters from the Holy Inquisition. But children and onlookers add a more boisterous note to the proceedings. Sorrow and joy walk hand in hand in Spain, and firecrackers pop, the anguished wail of a Gypsy song rises as certain statues pass by, and thousands of visitors watch from the sidelines, thrilled by the clamor of trumpets and drums and the gorgeous spectacle.

In the ancient city of Cartagena, tall hooded figures march in the Holy Week procession, a picture from the Middle Ages.

MUSEUM CITY:
SILENT
TOLEDO

FOR more than two thousand years a city has stood on this tawny hill above the swift-flowing Tagus (TAY-gus) River. Nearly the whole of Spanish history is encompassed in Toledo—Roman, Visigothic, Moslem and Christian—and many of the nation's treasures are to be seen here. In the sixteenth century the artist El Greco lived and worked here and his famous painting of the city is almost identical with the view of Toledo today.

Some of the earliest churches of the Visigoths became Moorish mosques, and when the town was recaptured in the eleventh century the mosques were converted to Christian churches again. The Jewish colony of Toledo was wealthy and powerful during the city's heyday, and several of their handsome synagogues were later reconstructed as churches too.

Toledo on its granite promontory, with the Tagus looping around three sides of it, looks like a fortress city hewn out of rock. An unusual silence hangs over the town, thanks to its Moorish builders who created a city of dark, twisting alleys, so steep and narrow that no traffic can move through them. Only donkeys and people on foot use the streets, and the Moorish houses rise straight up from them with forbidding walls, many of them windowless, while wrought iron gates bar the outsider from the delightful patios within.

The Cathedral of Toledo, whose tower dominates the skyline, and the other churches are filled with the magnificent handiwork of the city's ancient artisans. Toledo has been famous throughout its history for the quality of its steel blades and armor, and it is said, that the master armorers hardened their wonderfully flexible steel in the rushing waters of the Tagus. Toledo declined when the Court was moved to Madrid. Many of its industrious and wealthy citizens were Moors and Jews who were driven away during the Inquisition, a condition that further sapped the city's vitality. It is still an important ecclesiastical city, however, whose cardinal is the primate of Spain.

VINTAGE
FIESTA:
HARVEST
FESTIVAL

JEREZ de la Frontera (*heh-*
RETH *deh lah frohn-*TEH-*rah*)
near the southern Atlantic
coast of Spain is famous for its vineyards and the grapes they produce.

In the city of Jerez the liveliest celebration occurs during the Feast of the Vintage in the second week of September. Here, massed in front of one of the churches, is a group of young women of Jerez in their brilliant Andalusian costumes. If you look closely at the faces in this picture you will see evidence of British blood mixed with Andalusian. In the past century much of the local industry has been managed by the British, and Jerez has become partially Anglicized, adding still another strain to its fascinating mixture.

Spain is very much an agricultural country. More than half of all the workers in Spain work on the land. The typical farm is small and in many areas the same primitive farming methods are used now that were used hundreds of years ago. Irrigation, however, was introduced in southern Spain by the Moors more than a thousand years ago, and it is still important to the success of the crops.

Agricultural products vary because of the differences of climate in Spain which is a country of stormy mountain regions, a high, dry central plateau, and warm, fertile coastal plains.

The largest crop in Spain is wheat. Olives are probably next in importance. Olive trees can be grown on dry, hilly land that cannot be used for other things. Cork oaks are grown on hillsides, too, and the cork which comes from the thick bark of these trees is an important product of Spain. About one third of the world's supply of cork comes from these Spanish hillsides.

PALACE GARDEN: SPLENDOR IN GRANADA

FOR two hundred and fifty years Granada was the capital of the last Moors who remained in Spain. Little by little they had been forced from the land they had held, until only Granada remained to them. But of all their possessions in Spain the Moors loved Granada best. Even now, nearly five hundred years after their expulsion from this lovely valley, the loss of Granada is mourned in their evening prayers.

The Moorish kings were patrons of art, literature and science, and with their cultivated taste they built palaces that are masterpieces of Arabic architecture. The Alhambra (*ahl-*AHM-*brah*), a fortress palace set on a hill in Granada, and the nearby Generalife (*heh-neh-rah-*LEE-*feh*), a summer abode whose cool gardens we see here, are treasures beyond compare, left to Spain by her Moslem conquerors. The gardens and courtyards of the exotic palaces were not to the taste of Spanish kings and queens, and for many years the splendors of the Alhambra and Generalife were abandoned to beggars, Gypsies and stray dogs and cats. In 1829 the American author Washington Irving was captivated by the romance of the crumbling palace, where he lived surrounded by the ghosts of sultans and oriental dancing girls. His *Tales of the Alhambra* awoke Spain and the world to this Moorish miracle in Granada and as a result, the palaces and gardens have been restored to their former elegance for all to enjoy.

The Escorial, massive and severe, is the monastery-palace built by Philip II in 1584.

GRANADA GYPSIES: FLAMENCO DANCER

WHEN a Gypsy woman of Granada grows too old and fat to dance for a living she can be found at the Alhambra, peddling castanets, charms, flowers or photographs. The greasy-haired vendors whining and wheedling under the Moorish arches of the palace are a far cry from the fiery girls who can be seen on the opposite hill of the Albaicín (*ahl-by*-THEEN), the Gypsy quarter of Granada. Here, in whitewashed houses or in caves further up the hill, these colorful people have lived for four hundred years. Their costumes and music have become a vivid part of southern Spain.

The girl in this picture stands in the classic posture of the flamenco dancer. The Gypsies came originally from India, and it is said that the hands and arms of a flamenco dancer represent a hooded cobra or a crested peacock's head, swaying with hypnotic grace in patterns remembered from that far-off homeland. The clapping hands, the snapping fingers or rattling castanets, and the intricate foot-tapping that are

The wrinkled face of this old Gypsy still bears traces of her smouldering good looks.

part of this dance have their counterpart in the subtle rhythms of Hindu drummers. But the Spanish Gypsies have made this music their own, and they dance and sing with a flashing pride that is the essence of Spain. The best of the flamenco dancers have been truly great artists of world renown, but even the tawdriest display put on for tourists glows with the hidden fire that seems to be every Gypsy's birthright.

COURT OF THE LIONS: THE ALHAMBRA

IT IS DIFFICULT to conceive of Gypsies camping out in this delicate courtyard. But for many years, while the fragile mosaics and marbles were permitted to crumble and the water in pools and fountains grew stagnant, the stately Alhambra was a tenement for beggars. "Alhambra" comes from the Arabic word for red, and it is possible that the palace was given its name because of the reddish color of its walls. But a more dramatic likelihood is the fact that much of the construction was done by night when the hillside glowed red in the flares from hundreds of torches. The massive outer walls and ramparts of the citadel were built for defense. But the interior of the palace was planned to enhance all that was sweet and agreeable in life, and the filigree pavilions, slender columns and splashing fountains hint at the voluptuousness of the Moors.

The Court of Lions is at the heart of the Alhambra's living quarters, a quiet patio removed from the apartments of state, with the private halls and harem rooms opening from it. Twelve stylized lions circle a stone fountain, and in the heat and aridity of southern Spain this living water and its cool music added the final touch of luxury to the sultans' home. The shadows of the twelve lions have marked the passage of many hours upon the pavements of this court. And the strange stone beasts have been witness to countless intrigues and cruelties. The father of the last king of Granada married a beautiful Spanish slave girl who took the name Morning Star. His enraged queen encouraged their son to depose the old king, who then fled from the palace with Morning Star. Ten years later the son was forced to leave the Alhambra, too, when he handed over Granada to Ferdinand and Isabella. The gate through which he departed was sealed forever, and when the defeated king looked back at his Alhambra with a heartbroken sigh, his mother said bitterly, "Don't weep like a woman over what you could not hold like a man."

DOORMAN IN CORDOVA: MOORISH LEGACY

THE dashing costume of the Moorish horseman is seen no more in Spain, except as a fanciful uniform for hotel doormen or the like. Until recent years General Franco had a troop of Moorish guards, resplendently outfitted and mounted on Arabian steeds with gold-painted hoofs, but now even that faint echo of Islamic glory is gone. Here, in front of one of the new hotels in Cordova, the exotic past is given a modern revival, and visitors have a chance to see how the men looked who were responsible for the city's former greatness.

At the height of Moorish power in Spain, Cordova was one of Islam's most important capitals. In the ninth and tenth centuries the city had 800,000 inhabitants, 300 mosques and 600 inns. While Europe floundered through the Dark Ages, Cordova was illuminated by the most brilliant minds of its time. The precious heritage of knowledge that had been lost or forgotten when the barbarians overran Europe was carefully tended by the Moors in this city, and new ideas were born from the old. Philosophy, history, astronomy, geography, mathematics and medicine were all part of the rich intellectual ferment that seethed in Cordova. People came from darkened Europe for enlightenment and learning, and they brought back with them the continent's first knowledge of algebra, paper and glass, introduced at Cordova's university.

The Giralda tower at Seville, the Alhambra at Granada and the mosque at Cordova are the three greatest architectural legacies of the Moors. When Ferdinand III of Castile conquered Cordova in the thirteenth century, its citizens would not permit a stone of the glorious mosque to be touched. Instead they consecrated it as a Christian church just as it was. But in the sixteenth century the king gave his permission for a cathedral to be built within the mosque, and now a massive baroque church stands amidst the forest of slim Moorish columns. It is not the only anachronism in Cordova—as you can see in this picture—which for all its antiquity is one of the most progressive cities in Spain.

THE COSTA DEL SOL: HARBOR AT MALAGA

DUE south of Cordova, where the Mediterranean is a narrow arm between Africa and Spain, the Costa del Sol (*sohl*), or Sunny Coast, is dotted with charming port towns. The queen city of this coast is Málaga (MAH-*lah-gah*), a thriving resort and a prosperous seaport. Protected by mountains that rise to the north of it, Málaga has a balmy and relaxing climate with more hours of winter sunshine than any other city in Spain. Nature has been lavish here, and the town is like a glorious garden framed by palm trees, bamboos and giant eucalyptus trees. The Moors thought that Málaga "smelled like an open flask of musk," and certainly the streets of the town are perfumed by the daily flower markets where bouquets of roses, jasmine, carnations and camellias are for sale.

Along the twisting old streets you can hear the cries of girls selling oranges and the hoarse calls of fish vendors, for Málaga is also a big fishing port. The restaurants are famous for their special sea-food recipes, and along the beach there are any number of little eating places supplied with the fresh and abundant catch from boats like the one in this picture. Red millet and a kind of anchovy called *bouquerón* (*boo-keh-*ROHN) are the specialties rushed straight from the boat into the frying pan for a delicious waterfront treat. If you dine near the harbor at night you can see swarms of these little fishing smacks with their lights bobbing in the darkness.

Unusual long-handled dipper that reaches the bottom of a barrel

SMALL BUT MIGHTY: THE ROCK OF GIBRALTAR

THIS fortress rock is only a ten-mile ferryboat ride from Africa. In 711 when Tariq the Moor seized it and built the first fort here it became known as Jebel Tariq or Tariq's Mountain, and Gibraltar is a corruption of that name. Because of its strategic location at the narrow entrance to the Mediterranean—it was one of the two Pillars of Hercules in ancient times—Gibraltar has been a rock of contention through the ages. England has held it since 1713, and though it is only 2¼ square miles in area, this tiny Crown Colony has enormous importance.

On the upper Rock the famous Barbary apes, the only wild apes in Europe, sport happily on the heights. According to legend, as long as the apes remain on Gibraltar the Rock will belong to Britain. In the darkest days of World War II the ape colony dwindled alarmingly. Winston Churchill, ever the master strategist, gave orders to increase and maintain the monkey forces. After that was done the tide of war turned and now, when you see them, the Barbary apes look rather smug.

On an old monastery in Burgos the Cid rides forth heroically, emblem of Spanish chivalry.

Gibraltar is on a small peninsula joined to the southwest coast of Spain by a sandy plain. The towering Rock leaves little room for the town, and most visitors prefer to stay at Spanish Algeciras (*ahl-heh-*THEE-*rahs*) across the small bay. In a world that is changing so rapidly, it is a comfort to be in timeless Spain with a reassuring view of steadfast Gibraltar from your window.

SOME IMPORTANT DATES IN SPANISH HISTORY

c. 1000 B.C.	*Invasion of Celtic tribes from the north and Greek colonists along the Mediterranean coast.*
Sixth-second century B.C.	*Carthage controls the Iberian Peninsula.*
133 B.C.-Fifth century A.D.	*Rome rules the area known as Hispania. During this period Christianity is introduced.*
Fifth century	*Visigoths (or Western Goths) settle and rule until Moorish invasion of 711.*
711-1492	*Intermittent wars between Christian Spain and the Moors.*
1492	*Spain is unified through the marriage of the "Catholic Sovereigns," Ferdinand V and Isabella I; Granada, the last Moorish stronghold, falls; Columbus discovers America.*
Sixteenth century	*Golden Age. Wealth pours in from empire in America. Spain is the greatest power in Europe.*
1588	*Defeat of Spanish Armada by the British begins Spain's decline as a world power.*
1713	*War of the Spanish Succession ends with the recognition of Philip of Anjou as King of Spain. Beginning of Bourbon dynasty's rule in Spain.*
1808	*Napoleon invades Spain and places his brother Joseph Bonaparte on the Spanish throne.*
1808-1814	*War of Independence. Napoleon is defeated and Ferdinand VII is restored to the throne.*
1834	*Spanish Inquisition, begun in 1480, is permanently abolished by María Cristina.*
1870-75	*First Republic established under Prince Amadeo.*
1875-1931	*Bourbon rule re-established.*
1898	*Spanish-American War. By the Peace Treaty of Paris, Spain renounces all rights over Cuba and Puerto Rico, and cedes the Philippine Islands, the Sulus and the largest of the Marianas to the United States.*
1914-1918	*Spain remains neutral during World War I.*
1931	*Alfonso XIII abdicates after two decades of internal strife. Second Republican government is set up.*
July 17, 1936	*Army revolt in Spanish Morocco. General Francisco Franco lands in Spain and Civil War breaks out. Opponents of Left and Right are aided by Soviet Union, and Fascist Italy and Germany, respectively.*
March 31, 1939	*Civil War ends as Right-wing General Francisco Franco assumes rule.*
1939-1945	*Spain remains a nonbelligerent but supplies aid to the Fascist powers during early part of World War II.*
July, 1947	*The Law of Succession proclaims that Spain is a kingdom.*
1953	*Spain signs economic and military agreement with United States.*
1955	*Spain is admitted to the United Nations.*

SOME FAMOUS NAMES IN SPANISH HISTORY

THE CID (Rodrigo Díaz de Bivar) (1040?-1099)—*Soldier of fortune who captured Valencia from the Moors. His deeds inspired the epic* Poema del Cid.

MAIMONIDES (Rabbi Moses ben Maimon) (1135-1204)—*Jewish philosopher, physician, author. Notable works include the Hebrew* Mishneh Torah (Second Law) *and the Arabic* Guide of the Perplexed.

TOMAS DE TORQUEMEDA (1420-1498)—*Inquisitor general of Spain, noted as a fanatical hunter of heretics.*

FERDINAND (1452-1516) and ISABELLA (1451-1504)—*"The Catholic Sovereigns," whose marriage united Castile and Aragon. They financed the voyages of Columbus.*

JUAN PONCE DE LEON (1460?-1521)—*Discovered Florida while looking for the "Fountain of Perpetual Youth."*

VASCO NUNEZ DE BALBOA (1475-1517)—*Discovered the Pacific Ocean in 1513.*

FRANCISCO PIZARRO (1470?-1541)—*Conquered Inca Empire in Peru.*

ST. IGNATIUS OF LOYOLA (1491-1556)—*Founder of the Society of Jesus (Jesuits).*

CHARLES I (1500-1558)—*First ruling Hapsburg King in Spain. Also known as Charles V of the Holy Roman Empire.*

ST. FRANCIS XAVIER (1506-1552)—*Jesuit missionary to the Orient, known as the "Apostle of the Indies."*

ST. TERESA (1515-1582)—*Carmelite nun famous for her mystical visions. With St. John of the Cross, founded the order of barefoot Carmelites.*

MIGUEL DE CERVANTES (1547-1616)—*Spain's greatest literary figure, the creator of* Don Quixote.

EL GRECO, "The Greek" (Kyriakos Theotokopoulos) (1548?-1614? or 1625?)—*Master of mysticism in painting. Among his works are* View of Toledo, Crucifixion, Baptism of Christ.

LOPE DE VEGA (1562-1635)—*Soldier, priest, most popular writer of his day. Authored more than 2000 works and was the founder of Spanish dramatic comedy.*

DIEGO VELAZQUEZ (1599-1660)—*Leading exponent of naturalism in painting. His court paintings include portraits of Philip IV and Infanta María.*

JOSE CHURRIGUERA (1650-1723)—*Architect and sculptor. Developed an ornate variation of the baroque style, now called Churrigueresque.*

PHILIP V (1683-1746)—*Founded Bourbon dynasty in Spain. His accession to the throne in 1701 marks the beginning of the War of Spanish Succession.*

FRANCISCO GOYA (1746-1828)—*Court painter, etcher and lithographer. His realistic paintings of the royal family and political scenes resulted in his exile.*

MANUEL DE FALLA (1876-1946)—*Composer, whose works include the* Fire Dance *and the ballet* The Three-Cornered Hat.

PABLO PICASSO (1881-   )—*Leading contemporary artist, and founder of Cubism.*

JOSE ORTEGA Y GASSET (1883-1955)—*Philosopher, writer and statesman.*

GENERAL FRANCISCO FRANCO (1892-   )—*Dictator of Spain. Assumed powers on March 28, 1939.*

JOAN MIRO (1893-   )—*Painter, sculptor and engraver, identified with highly imaginative, sometimes humorous school of art.*

FEDERICO GARCIA LORCA (1898-1936)—*Andalusian poet and playwright, killed during Civil War.*

SALVADOR DALI (1904-   )—*Artist known for his dreamlike surrealist paintings.*

SOME SPANISH WORDS AND PHRASES

English	Spanish
Do you speak English?	¿Habla usted inglés? (AH-*blah* oos-TEHD *een*-GLEHS)
How do you say—?	¿Cómo se dice—? (KOH-*moh seh* DEE-*theh*—)
Can you help me?	¿Puede ayudarme? (PWEH-*deh ah-yoo*-DAHR-*meh*)
I do not understand.	No comprendo. (*noh kohm*-PREHN-*doh*)
Please.	Por favor. (*pohr fah*-VOHR)
Hello (Good day).	Buenos días. (BWEH-*nohs* DEE-*ahs*)
Good-by.	Adiós. (*ah*-DYOHS)
How much (is it)?	¿Cuánto cuesta? (KWAHN-*toh* KWEHS-*tah*)
Many thanks.	Muchas gracias. (MOO-*chahs* GRAH-*thyahs*)
You are welcome (Don't mention it).	De nada. (*deh* NAH-*dah*)
Where is—?	¿Dónde está—? (DOHN-*deh ehs*-TAH—)

Airport	Aeropuerto (*ah-eh-roh*-PWEHR-*toh*)	Airplane	Avión (*ah*-VYOHN)
Bus	Autobus (*ow-toh*-BOOS)	Train	Tren (*trehn*)
Boat	Barco (BAHR-*koh*)	Baggage	Equipaje (*eh-kee*-PAH-*heh*)
Hotel	Hotel (*oh*-TEHL)	Station	Estación (*ehs-tah*-THYOHN)
Meat	Carne (KAHR-*neh*)	Eggs	Huevos (WEH-*vohs*)
Fish	Pescado (*pehs*-KAH-*doh*)	Coffee	Café (*kah*-FEH)
Water	Agua (AH-*gwah*)	Milk	Leche (LEH-*cheh*)
Today	Hoy (*oy*)	Yesterday	Ayer (*ah*-YEHR)
Tonight	Esta noche (EHS-*tah* NOH-*cheh*)	Tomorrow	Mañana (*mah*-NYAHN-*nah*)
Week	Semana (*seh*-MAH-*nah*)	Month	Mes (*mehs*)
Night	Noche (NOH-*cheh*)	Year	Año (AH-*nyoh*)

DAYS OF THE WEEK:

Monday	Lunes (LOO-*nehs*)
Tuesday	Martes (MAHR-*tehs*)
Wednesday	Miércoles (MYEHR-*koh-lehs*)
Thursday	Jueves (HWEH-*vehs*)
Friday	Viernes (VYEHR-*nehs*)
Saturday	Sábado (SAH-*bah-doh*)
Sunday	Domingo (*doh*-MEEN-*goh*)

NUMBERS:

One	Uno (OO-*noh*)	Seven	Siete (SYEH-*teh*)
Two	Dos (*dohs*)	Eight	Ocho (OH-*choh*)
Three	Tres (*trehs*)	Nine	Nueve (NWEH-*veh*)
Four	Cuatro (KWAH-*troh*)	Ten	Diez (DYEHTH)
Five	Cinco (THEEN-*koh*)	One Hundred	Cien (THYEHN)
Six	Seis (SEH-*ees*)	One Thousand	Mil (*meel*)

MONEY:

Peseta (*peh*-SEH-*tah*)

Duro (DOO-*roh*)	5 pesetas (the "piece-of-eight" in pirate stories)
Centimo (THEHN-*tee-moh*)	1/100 of a peseta

INDEX

Africa, 9, 11, 57, 78
Agriculture, 66
Albaicín, 70
Alcazar, 38
Alfonso VI, 41
Alfonso XII, 18
Algeciras, 78
Alhambra, 69, 70, 73, 74
Alicante, 57
Altamira, 10, 29
America, 11
Anchovy, 77
Andalusia, 13, 25, 58, 61, 66
Aqueduct, 37
Arabian Nights, 58
Aragon, 11, 13
Architecture, 37, 46, 74
Arco de Santa María, 34
Armada, Invincible, 12
Armor, 65
Art, 10, 22, 29, 65
Asturias, 11, 13
Avila, 41, 42
Balboa, Vasco Nunez de, 81
Balearic Islands, 50
Barbary Apes, 78
Barber of Seville, 58
Barcelona, 13, 42, 45, 46
Basques, 13, 26
Bay of Biscay, 26
Beaches, 26, 42, 50, 57, 77
Benidorm, 57
Berbers, 11, 25

Black Virgin, 49
Bonaparte, Joseph, 12
Bouquerón, 77
Bourbons, 12
Bridge of Santa María, 34
Britain, 78
British, 66
Bullfighting, 21, 61
Burgos, 34, 78
Caballero, 12
Cadiz, 14
Cafés, 14, 18, 26
Campus Stellae, 30
Carmen, 58, 61
Carpets, 22
Cartagena, 62
Carthaginians, 10
Castile, 11, 14, 25, 29, 34, 38, 41
Castles, 13, 38
Catalans, 13
Catalonia, 13, 42, 45, 46, 49
Cathedrals, 30, 34, 58, 65, 74
Caves, 9, 29, 50
Celts, 10, 38
Cervantes, Miguel de, 16, 33, 81
Charles V, 34, 81
Charros, 61
Chopin, Frederic, 53
Christians, 11, 30, 41
Churches, 30, 34, 46, 58, 65, 74
Churchill, Winston, 78
Churriguera, Jose, 81
Cid, The, 34, 78, 81

Civil Guards, 53
Civil War, 12, 16
Columbus, Christopher, 11, 34, 38, 45, 49
Communism, 12
Compostela, 30
Cordova, 14, 74
Cork, 66
Costa Blanca, 57
Costa Brava, 42
Costa del Sol, 77
Costumes, 25, 53, 61, 66, 74
Court of Lions, 73
Cowboys, 61
Dali, Salvador, 9, 46, 81
Dances, 25, 53, 61, 70
Dates in Spanish History, 80
Devil's Bridge, 37
Don Giovanni, 58
Don Quixote, 16, 33
Dragon Caves, 50
Edificio España, 16
Escolania, 49
Escorial, 69
Estremadura, 13
Fairs, 61
Falla, Manuel de, 81
Fallas, 54
Farming, 66
Fascism, 12
Feast of the Vintage, 66
Ferdinand, 11, 34, 45, 73, 81
Ferdinand III, 58, 74
Feria, 61
Festivals, 25, 66
Fiestas, 54
"Fifth Column," 16
Fishing, 42, 77
Flamenco, 70
Franco, Francisco, 12, 74, 81
Franks, 45
Galicia, 13, 30
Gaudí, Antonio, 46
Generalife, 69
Geography, 9
Gibraltar, 78
Gibraltar, Strait of, 9
Gil Blas, 29
Giralda, 58, 74
Goya, Francisco, 10, 22, 81
Granada, 11, 69, 70
Gran Via, 16

Greco, El, 10, 65, 81
Greeks, 10, 45
Gregorian chants, 49
Gypsies, 61, 70
Hadrian, 10
Hannibal, 45
Hapsburgs, 12, 34
Hispania, 10, 37
History, 9, 10, 11, 12, 80, 81
Holy Family, 46
Holy Week, 62
Iberian Peninsula, 9
Iberians, 38
Inquisition, 11, 62, 65
Irrigation, 66
Irving, Washington, 69
Isabella, 11, 34, 38, 45, 73, 81
Islam, 11, 25, 74
Islands, Balearic, 50
Jebel Tariq, 78
Jerez de la Frontera, 66
Jesuits, 49
Jews, 65
Judea, 30
Juvenal, 10
La Concha, 26
La Mancha, 33
Lagartera, 25
Langostinos, 57
La Granja, 38
Language, 10, 13, 14, 82
León, 11, 14
Lions, Court of, 73
Literature, 16, 29, 33, 34
Lorca, Federico Garcia, 81
Low Countries, 12
Loyola, Ignatius, 49, 81
Madrid, 14, 16, 18
Madrileños, 16, 18
Maimonides, 81
Majorca, 50, 53
Málaga, 77
Map, 6
Martial, 10
Mary Tudor, 18
Matador, 21
Mediterranean Sea, 10, 42, 50, 57, 77, 78
Middle Ages, 30, 34, 62
Minaret, 58
Miro, Joan, 81
Monasteries, 29, 49, 53, 69

Montserrat, 46, 49
Moors, 11, 13, 25, 30, 34, 41, 58, 65, 66,
   69, 74
Morning Star, 73
Moslems, 11
Mosques, 65, 74
Mountains, 9, 49
Music, 49, 53, 70
Names in Spanish History, 81
Napoleon, 9
Nationalists, 12
Navarre, 13
New World, 12, 45, 49
Numantia, 10
Olives, 66
Ortega y Gasset, Jose, 81
Paella, 57
Painting, 10, 22, 29, 65
Palaces, 69, 73
Palma, 50
Park, Retiro, 18
Pasos, 62
Penitents, 62
Peñon de Ifach, 57
Philip II, 18, 69
Philip V, 38, 81
Phoenicians, 10
Picasso, Pablo, 10, 46, 81
Pigeon Shooting, 26
Pillars of Hercules, 78
Pizarro, Francisco, 81
Plaza de España, 16
Plaza de Toros, 21
Ponce de Leon, Juan, 81
Portugal, 9
Prado, 16
Prawns, 57
Prehistoric Era, 9, 29
Punic Wars, 10
Pyrenees, 9
Ramblas, 45
Red Millet, 77
Republicans, 12
Resorts, 26, 42, 50, 57, 77
Retiro Park, 18
Rice, 57
"Riviera of the Future," 42
Rock of Gibraltar, 78
Romans, 10, 37, 38, 45
Sagrada Familia, 46
St. Francis Xavier, 81
St. Ignatius of Loyola, 49, 81

St. James, 30
St. Joseph, 54
St. Luke, 49
St. Peter, 49
Sancho Panza, 16, 33
Sand, George, 53
San Sebastián, 26
Santa Barbara, 22
Santa Juliana, 29
Santa María (saint), 34
Santa María (ship), 45
Santa Teresa, 41, 81
Santiago de Compostela, 30
Santillana del Mar, 29
Segovia, 37, 38
Seneca, 10
Seville, 58, 61, 62
Sierras, 41
Sitges, 46
Skin Diving, 50
Spanish rice, 57
Sports, 21, 26
Stone Age, 9
Strait of Gibraltar, 9
"Suit of Lights," 21
Sunny Coast, 77
Tagus River, 65
Tales of the Alhambra, 69
Tapestries, 22
Tariq, 11, 78
Toledo, 14, 65
Torero, 21
Torquemeda, de, Tomas, 81
Tossa de Mar, 42
Trajan, 10
Valencia, 34, 54, 57
Valldemosa, 53
Vega, Lope de, 81
Velásquez, Diego, 10, 81
Versailles, 38
Vineyards, 66
Vintage, Feast, 66
Visigoths, 10, 13, 65
War, Civil, 12, 16
War, World, II, 78
Weathervane, 58
Weaving, 22
Wheat, 66
White Coast, 57
Windmills, 33
Words and Phrases, 82
World War II, 78